Soulful Departure
End-of-Life Readiness

A Comprehensive Guide and Workbook

SUSAN DAVID

INDIA · SINGAPORE · MALAYSIA

Copyright © Susan David 2024
All Rights Reserved.

ISBN 979-8-89415-399-5

This book has been published with all efforts taken to make the material error-free after the consent of the author. However, the author and the publisher do not assume and hereby disclaim any liability to any party for any loss, damage, or disruption caused by errors or omissions, whether such errors or omissions result from negligence, accident, or any other cause.

While every effort has been made to avoid any mistake or omission, this publication is being sold on the condition and understanding that neither the author nor the publishers or printers would be liable in any manner to any person by reason of any mistake or omission in this publication or for any action taken or omitted to be taken or advice rendered or accepted on the basis of this work. For any defect in printing or binding the publishers will be liable only to replace the defective copy by another copy of this work then available.

Part A: Guide Book

Susan David

Contents

Embarking on Eternity

As I delve into the realm of mortality, I find myself waltzing through a delicate balance of curiosity, apprehension and a profound sense of wonder. Death, often shrouded in mystery, is an inevitable chapter in our narrative—a universal reality we all share. It evokes a spectrum of emotions and reflections, each as distinctive as the individual harboring them.

My quest to understand death has allowed me to see it not merely as a cessation but as an integral facet of the beautiful tapestry of life. The shadow gives depth to the light, the silence punctuates the melody. And within this contemplation, I unearth a certain beauty— an acceptance that life's transient nature adds a precious hue to every fleeting moment.

How do you perceive the interplay between life and death in your own existence?

There is humility in acknowledging the ephemeral nature of our existence against the expansive canvas of the cosmos. It is a gentle reminder to cherish the richness of experience, forge meaningful bonds and embark on soulful adventures. The cognizance of our mortality, far from being morbid, ignites a purposeful and deliberate journey through life.

Yet, beyond the philosophical realm, the pragmatic facets of death await our attention. The logistics of mortality—wills, funeral arrangements and more—stand as testaments to our duty towards those who will continue the journey in our absence. While sometimes uncomfortable, addressing these tasks can be an expression of love and consideration for those we hold dear.

Have you initiated steps to address the practical aspects of your mortality?

Guide to Navigate this Journal:

This journal comprises two (2) parts: Part A serves as a comprehensive guidebook, while Part B functions as a practical workbook. Structured as a step-by-step manual, it empowers readers to navigate each section of the workbook at their own pace, using the guidebook in Part A as a reference.

Featuring detailed explanations, checklists and sample templates, this journal serves as a valuable resource for individuals and families, simplifying the often-overwhelming task of end-of-life planning.

Chapter I

A Checklist for Executors – What to do when someone dies?

Embarking on the journey of bidding a final farewell to a loved one is a path filled with emotions, memories and responsibilities. As we navigate through the sorrow of loss, there rests upon our shoulders the crucial task of ensuring their wishes are honored and their affairs are handled with utmost care and respect.

The role of an executor is a significant one, often appointed due to trust, capability and a deep understanding of the deceased person's wishes. As an executor, you are entrusted with the responsibility of managing the final affairs, which includes a spectrum of tasks from notifying the appropriate entities and safeguarding assets, to orchestrating the funeral arrangements.

This checklist is curated to provide a structured roadmap to guide you through the essential tasks that need to be addressed promptly and diligently. Each item on the checklist is a step towards honoring the life lived, making the process a little less daunting during a time of grief.

As you proceed through this checklist, each step you take is a tribute to the life and wishes of the deceased. Your meticulous efforts, although challenging, are a profound testament to your love and dedication.

Here is a simplified breakdown of the tasks that lie ahead:

Disclaimer: While this checklist aims to provide general guidance applicable in various circumstances, it is essential to be aware that legal and cultural aspects related to end-of- life matters may vary by country or region. Readers are encouraged to seek local advice or consult with professionals familiar with the specific jurisdiction to ensure accurate and appropriate actions.

Immediate Steps Following a Loss: Essential Actions to Undertake Without Delay

1. **Formal Acknowledgment: Initiating the Legal Pronouncement of Death**

   Obtaining an official declaration of death, usually from a medical professional or coroner.

2. **Gift of Life: Exploring Organ Donation Options (if applicable)**

   Ensuring timely communication with the relevant authorities if the deceased opted for organ donation. **Disclaimer:** Organ donation procedures and regulations can differ significantly based on jurisdiction and available medical facilities. The information provided here serves as a general guide, and readers are advised to consult with local healthcare authorities or relevant organizations for specific guidelines in their area.

3. **Informing Close Connections: Communicating the Loss to Loved Ones**

Communicating the somber news to family and close friends about the passing.

4. **Arrangements for the Departed: Managing Body Disposition and Transportation**

Making arrangements for the body's collection and transportation as per the deceased's pre-arranged plans or wishes.

5. **Ensuring Care for Loved Ones: Pet and Dependent Care Arrangements**

Ensuring immediate care for any dependents or pets of the deceased.

6. **Safeguarding Assets: Protocols for Securing Major Properties**

Securing the deceased's residence and vehicles, and informing relevant parties in case the property will be vacant for an extended period.

7. **Workplace Communication: Informing the Employer of the Individual's Passing**

In the event that the departed individual was employed, make a notification call to inform the relevant organization about their passing. Use this opportunity to inquire about outstanding payments, benefits and life insurance details.

Timely Tasks in the Aftermath: Essential Steps to Take Within the First Few Days

8. **Funeral Arrangements: Thoughtful Decision-Making for Memorial Services**

    Facilitating funeral arrangements in accordance with the deceased's pre-established plans or collaborating with a funeral home in the absence of such plans is crucial. Seek guidance from a funeral director to explore options, including immediate burial or cremation.

    Kindly refer to Chapter IV: Funeral Planning

Guiding Preparations for Commemorative Events: Actions Leading Up to the Funeral, Memorial Service or Celebration of Life

9. **Evaluating Financial Needs: Assessing the Requirement for Assistance**

    The expenses associated with a funeral can be a significant burden for many families. While there are various ways to minimize costs, exploring financial assistance from government aid, family and friends is also worth considering. For example, in Malaysia, the Death Assistance is a gesture of compassion by the Employees Provident Fund (EPF) to our member's next-of-kin (under EPF's discretion). A one-time payment of RM2,500 will be considered and awarded to any of the deceased member's eligible dependents. (widow/widower, child or member's parents subject to member's marital status).

Source: https://www.kwsp.gov.my/member/account-centre/death. Meanwhile, crowdfunding campaigns for funerals are increasingly common in selected parts of the world.

10. Curating Funeral Participation: Thoughtful Selection of Ceremony Contributors

When inviting friends or family members to participate in funeral activities, initiate open communication and discuss the specific roles and their involvement in these activities proactively.

11. Establishing the Funeral Timeline: Crafting a Thoughtful Schedule for the Ceremony

Establish the timing and venue for all events, including structured activities.

Key Tasks in the Weeks Following: Essential Actions to Undertake

12. Contacting Life Insurance Providers: Initiating Notification

Procedures Complete the required claim forms for the deceased's life insurance policies and advise friends and family who may have named the deceased as a beneficiary in their life, health, car or homeowner's insurance policies to review and update their information. For each insurance company, visit the official website to understand the specific process and proceed accordingly. Alternatively, seek expert guidance to ensure a thorough and accurate handling of the procedures.

13. Notify the Social Security Office

You can apply for survivor benefits through your country's Social Security system if applicable. Visit the official website to understand the specific process and find any required forms, as the details may vary by country.

14. Notify Banks and Mortgage Companies

Refer to Chapter 2, 'My Banking Details,' in this journal for relevant information. Provide copies of the death certificate to each bank for the seamless transfer of account ownership and the cancellation of credit cards. In instances where access to a safe deposit box is required without an available key, securing a court order may be essential for opening and inventorying its contents. It is crucial to recognize that these procedures may differ by country; thus, seeking guidance from a local expert or authority is advisable.

15. Manage Essential Payments: Identify and Settle Important Bills

This information can be obtained in Chapter 2, of this journal under "My Banking Details". In situations where the deceased lived alone without family, create a list of expected bills like mortgage, car payments and utilities by accessing information from their mail and online accounts. Ensure the necessary steps are taken to disconnect utility services. Regarding loans, this is associated with Task #14 (Notify Banks and Mortgage Companies). Always refer to the official website of the respective departments or seek expert guidance to complete this task, as procedures may vary from country to country.

16. Finalize Digital Presence: Close Email Accounts and Terminate All Subscriptions

This information can be obtained in Chapter 2, of this journal under "Services to Close and Cancel". When you are assured that you have acquired the required information from other accounts, consider permanently closing your loved one's email accounts as an extra measure to prevent fraud and identity theft. Each email provider has its own process, so conduct a quick online search to determine the specific steps you need to take.

17. Initiate Probate Proceedings with the Will

If the estate is modest in size, lacks unusual assets and is not anticipated to face disputes among family members, you might consider managing it independently. Nevertheless, it is advisable to evaluate whether engaging a probate lawyer would be beneficial in navigating the process more effectively.

Chapter II

Journal Owner – Who am I?

In a world increasingly intertwined with digital threads, the significance of safeguarding our personal and sensitive information has soared. Documenting vital details about ourselves is a prudent step, not only for our peace of mind but also for the ease and security of our loved ones in unforeseen circumstances. This chapter, "Journal Owner: Who Am I?", is designed to be a safe harbor where you can anchor crucial information about yourself, crafting a reliable reference for the future.

However, with the boon of information comes the bane of potential misuse. The details penned down in this section are delicate and if fallen into the wrong hands, could be misused in ways detrimental to you and your loved ones. Hence, it is paramount that this journal is kept in a secure and safe location, accessible only to trusted individuals. Be it a locked safe, a secure digital vault or a trusted confidant, choose a sanctuary for this journal that stands robust against unauthorized access.

As you fill out the ensuing pages, you are not merely jotting down facts; you are creating a shield, a legacy of protection for yourself and your loved ones. Each piece of information is a brick in the fortress of your life's security. Handle it with the diligence, caution and care it warrants, for in the right hands, this information is a torch guiding the way through the fog of uncertainty, but in the wrong hands, it could be a storm battering against the fortress you strive to build.

Note: The information listed below is essential or standard for your executor, but you have the option to offer additional details to facilitate the process. For instance, in the Insurance Details column, you may choose to include your agent's contact number if desired.

A. Personal Details:

- Full Legal Name: ___________________________

- Date of Birth: _____________________

- International Passport Number: ____________________________

- National Identification Number: ___________________________

- Current Residential Address: _________________________

- Personal Mobile Number: ____________________________

- Personal Email Address: _______________________________

Social Security Details (Applicable for Malaysians):

- Employees Provident Fund (EPF) Number: ______________

- Social Security Organization (SOCSO) Number: ___________

Insurance Details:

Review and update beneficiaries on insurance policies. (attach as an annexure to the original Will document for reference)

- Personal Insurance Provider Name: _______________________

- Policy Number (if any): _______________________

Employment Information:

- Current Employer Name: _______________________

- Current Employer HR Contact Details: _______________________

B. Important Contacts:

Provide a comprehensive list of crucial contacts, including family members, lawyers, financial advisors and healthcare providers, facilitating communication and coordination during the execution of your plans.

Spouse Details:

- Full Legal Name: _______________________

- Contact Details: _______________________

Children Details (Repeat for each child):

- Full Legal Name: _______________________

- Contact Details: _______________________

Support System Mapping: Guardian / Best Friend Details/ Tribe:

Tribe refers to different group of friends from school, college, work, clubs etc. where a representative detail is required for communication purposes.

- Full Legal Name: _______________________________

- Relationship: _________________________________

- Contacts Details: _______________________________

- Institute Engaged (Name): _____________________

C. Medical Information:

- Blood Group: [ ] O+ [ ] O- [ ] A+ [ ] A- [ ] B+ [ ] B- [ ] AB+ [ ] AB-

While comprehensive medical records may not appear essential posthumously, certain key medical-related details could prove beneficial for your designated executor, particularly in the context of unforeseen circumstances such as a death resulting from negligence, which may give rise to legal considerations. These details may include information like allergies, medication lists, chronic diseases, immunization history and others.

D. Important Documents:

Ensure precise organization and easy access to vital documents for the effective execution of your will and estate planning.

This section offers practical tips and a checklist of essential documents that need to be compiled, including specifying their storage locations. Chapter 3 of this journal provides guidance on securely storing these documents while maintaining accessibility.

Primary Documents:

- Original Copy of Official Will Document

- Original Copy of Advance Directive Form (varies by country and jurisdiction)

- Password Sheet (securely stored)

- Original Copy of National Identification Card

- Copy of National Identification Card (it is essential to retain in case the original document is lost or unavailable at the time of death)

- Original Copy of International Passport (it is essential to cancel the passport to avoid fraud)

- Copy of International Passport (it is essential to retain in case the original document is lost)

- Printed Copy of Social Security Fund Nominees / Beneficiary Details

  Review and update beneficiaries on Social Security Fund. (attach as an annexure to the original Will document for reference)

- Original Copy of Personal Insurance Policies (if any)

- Original Copies of Bank Mortgage Documents

- Original Copies of other Financial Investment Documents (shares, unit trust, crypto- currency etc.)

  Review and update beneficiaries on Financial Investment. (attach as an annexure to the original Will document for reference)

- Company-owned Contracts / Documents

- Children's Documentation (Birth Certificate / National Identification Card, Medical Records, School Records, Certificates etc.) Note: Children below 18 years old

- Marriage Certificates

- Divorce Documents

Supplementary Documents:

- Original Copy of Birth Certificate

- Original Copies of Education Certifications

- Medical History Reports (including organ donor card, blood donation book etc.)

- Current Employer Offer Letter

- Vehicle Records

- Pet License and Medical Records

- Tax Returns

E. Where to Find My...:

Please mention where the related documents (if any) are stored

- House Keys (including spare keys)

- Vehicle Keys (including spare keys)

- Wallet / Purse / Card Holders

- Safe Deposit / Jewelry Box

- Memory Box

- Arts / Collectible Items

F. My Pets Information (if any):

Review and update beneficiaries on Pet caretaker (attach as an annexure to the original Will document for reference)

- Pet Name

- Beneficiary / Caretaker (optional, you may choose to specify here or directly within the Will document)

- Other Details (e.g.: Insurance Policies or Savings Accounts registered in the pet's name)

G. My Estate Custodian:

Confidential Information: Please refrain from sharing sensitive data, such as bank login credentials, in this session

Ensuring a precise documentation of your assets and liabilities is essential for the accurate implementation of your will and estate planning. This section meticulously leads you through the process of enumerating your assets and liabilities, providing templates and guidance to facilitate the creation of a comprehensive and transparent financial overview for the benefit of your executors and beneficiaries.

- Property Name

- Property Address

- Financial Institution / Corporate Affiliation (Name and Branch)

- Monthly Mortgage Payment

- Home Mortgage Account Number

H. My Vehicle:

Confidential Information: Please refrain from sharing sensitive data, such as bank login credentials, in this session

- Vehicle Registration Number / Model

- Financial Institution / Corporate Affiliation (Name and Branch)

- Monthly Mortgage Payment

- Vehicle Mortgage Account Number

I. My Banking Details:

Confidential Information: Please refrain from sharing sensitive data, such as bank login credentials, in this session

- Credit Card Account Details / Bank

- Savings Account Details / Bank

- Current Account Details / Bank

- Fixed Deposit Account Details / Bank

- Joint Account Details / Bank

- Home Mortgage Account Details / Bank

- Vehicle Mortgage Account Details / Bank

- Personal Loan Account Details / Bank

- Bank Safe Box Details / Bank

- Other Investment Account Details (applicable in your respective country)

  These investment accounts are tailored for residents in Malaysia, adhering to specific regulatory frameworks and offerings available exclusively to Malaysian citizens. Feel free to provide details of any other investment accounts applicable in your country, as illustrated in the example below. Example:

- Amanah Saham Nasional Berhad (ASNB) Investment Account Details

- Public Mutual Investment Account Details

- Kenanga Investment Account Details

J. Services to Close and Cancel:

Confidential Information: Please refrain from sharing sensitive data, such as bank login credentials, in this session

List down subscriptions/memberships with automated debit arrangements.

Note: To close a Gmail account, Google provides a tool known as 'Inactive Account Manager.' To access it, go to your Google account settings. This tool allows the account owner to designate individuals with whom they wish to share information in the event of their passing. Users can select up to 10 people for this purpose.

Subscriptions / Memberships	YES (name the subscriptions)	NO
Primary Gmail Account (registered for all financial related matters)		

Subscriptions / Memberships	YES (name the subscriptions)	NO
Mobile Subscription		
Internet Subscription		
Utilities – Electric		
Utilities – Water		
Television Subscription (Amazon Prime, Disney+, Netflix, Apple / Android TV etc.)		
Home Security – Alarm & CCTV		
Home Appliances – Water Filter, Air Purifier, Smart Home Appliances etc.		
Digital Payment (Google Pay, Apple Pay, Samsung Pay etc.)		
Crypto-currency		
Gym / Sports Club Membership		
Premium Car Wash Membership		

Subscriptions / Memberships	YES (name the subscriptions)	NO
LinkedIn (Premier)		
Spotify (Premier)		
YouTube (Premier)		
Newspaper		
Other Subscriptions (Magazines, AI Tools, Learning Portals etc.)		

Active Social Media Subscriptions		
Kindly state who should have the access to the below listed social media accounts and what should be done with each account.		
Facebook		
Instagram		
WhatsApp		
Twitter		
TikTok		
Snapchat		
eBay		

Active Social Media Subscriptions		
Pinterest		
Telegram		
Others		

K. Digital Assets:

In the age of technological evolution, our lives are intricately woven into a digital tapestry, comprising websites, online stores (e.g., Shopify, Etsy) and digital portfolios (e.g., Dribbble, Teachable). These digital assets, often overlooked in traditional end-of-life preparations, hold a unique value that extends beyond the physical realm.

As we embark on a journey to ensure our legacy lives on, understanding how to securely unlock and transfer these digital treasures becomes paramount. It is important to provide secure access instructions for these assets. Below are some tips to ensure secure access to your digital assets:

1. Utilize robust passwords and regularly update them (e.g., incorporate symbols, numbers, with a mix of upper and lower case). This practice enhances the security of your accounts, minimizing the risk of unauthorized access.

2. Enhance security by enabling two-factor authentication (2FA) (e.g., receiving a code on your phone in addition

to entering a password). This additional layer of security enhances the protection of your accounts.

Understanding the meticulous documentation of access instructions is essential, facilitating the designated executor in carrying out your wishes posthumously. Utilize the guidelines provided in Chapter III: Password Sheet for structured documentation options with a focus on high security. It is imperative to furnish specific and clear instructions for each respective asset to mitigate the risk of confusion and ensure the accurate execution of your directives.

Here are additional recommendations for securely accessing digital assets while utilizing public Wi-Fi networks:

1. Safeguard data on public Wi-Fi by using a Virtual Private Network (VPN) (e.g., ExpressVPN, NordVPN) to encrypt your internet traffic, rendering it more challenging for hackers to intercept your data.

2. Refrain from accessing sensitive information, such as online banking accounts when using public Wi-Fi.

3. When utilizing public Wi-Fi, deactivate file sharing on your device to prevent other individuals on the network from accessing your files.

Chapter III

Password Sheet – Keys to the Virtual Kingdom

As we transition from securing individual digital assets explored in the previous chapter, the focus shifts to the Password Sheet. This chapter outlines a systematic approach to managing passwords for social media, email and digital wallets. It proposes tailored solutions for secure storage and controlled sharing, ensuring a seamless continuation from safeguarding digital treasures to the comprehensive protection of our online legacy. The Password Sheet emerges as the conductor, orchestrating a harmonious transition into the digital afterlife.

Password Managers:

- Embrace software like LastPass, Dashlane or 1Password, constructing an encrypted vault accessible through a single master password. These tools transcend geographical boundaries, designed for a global user base.

Hardware Security Keys:

- Equip yourself with devices like YubiKey or Google Titan Security Key, offering a physical method for secure two-factor authentication and password management. These keys know no geographical constraints, ensuring global usability.

Offline Password Vaults:

- Users could opt for offline password managers like KeePassXC which store password information on the user's local machine rather than on the cloud, providing an extra layer of control.

Secure Digital Note-Taking Applications:

- Applications like Evernote or Microsoft OneNote with robust encryption features can be used to store password information securely, provided they are locked behind strong, unique passwords.

Encrypted Digital Vaults:

- Software like VeraCrypt allows users to create encrypted digital vaults on their computers where they can securely store passwords and other sensitive information.

Encrypted USB Drives:

- Storing password information on a hardware-encrypted USB drive that requires a pin or biometric authentication can also be a secure alternative.

Secure Cloud Storage Services:

- Utilizing cloud storage services with robust encryption like Tresorit or pCloud for storing an encrypted password vault.

Paper-Based Password Notebooks:

- Although not digital, a physical notebook stored in a highly secure location like a safe deposit box is a traditional yet effective method of password management.

Biometric Password Managers:

- Solutions that use fingerprint or facial recognition technology to secure a digital password vault, providing a balance of convenience and security.

Multi-Factor Authentication (MFA):

- While not a password management solution per se, enabling MFA wherever possible adds an additional layer of security which can be crucial in protecting digital assets.

Chapter IV

Funeral Planning – A Symphony of Final Wishes

Embarking on the journey of funeral planning transcends cultural and religious boundaries. This chapter is not just a guide; it is a thoughtful overture, a prelude to orchestrating your final rites in a manner that resonates with your essence, offering solace to loved ones during times of sorrow.

1. **Designate a Responsible Individual to Contact Religious Leaders and Funeral Services Company:**

   Designate a responsible individual to liaise with religious leaders, ensuring that your spiritual preferences are honored in the organization of your funeral. This appointed steward can also extend invitations to preferred religious leaders to conduct your final rites.

2. **Harmony in Funeral Services: Crafting the Farewell:**

   Conduct thorough research to select the funeral services provider of your choice for the meticulous organization of your funeral arrangements. This encompasses essential tasks such as the option of embalming or dry ice preservation, cosmetology procedures, burial/cremation preference and dressing requirements. Additionally, if deemed necessary, coordinate the publication of an obituary in the local newspaper. Include comprehensive contact details in Part B: Work Book, specifying your preferences for arranging wake and funeral services.

3. **Venue Selection: Choosing the Stage for the Final Act:**

Choose your preferred funeral parlor or family home and cemetery. Choosing the venue is a crucial step in the planning process. The right funeral home will honor your wishes and provide support to your family during a difficult time.

4. **Resting in Peace: Burial or Cremation:**

Burial and cremation are the two primary methods for laying a person to rest. Each option has its own set of rituals, costs and considerations.

4.1 **If Choosing Burial, please specify:**

- For a new lot

- OR pick your preferred existing grave (if any)

For example: To be interred in my late grandmother's grave in my hometown

4.2 **If Opting for Cremation, please indicate your preference for the ashes:**

- To be buried in a new lot

- To be placed in one's grave

- To be enshrined in a stupa or other sacred structures at your residence

- To be scattered in a specific ocean (name the ocean)

- To be shared with loved ones (provide names)

- Other suggestions

5. **Casket Choices: Crafting the Vessel for the Voyage Beyond:**

Pick your casket design, material and color according to your preferences, budget constraints and any environmental or cultural considerations. It is advisable to consult the chosen funeral service provider (point #2) to explore available options and make an informed decision based on your needs and values. For example:

- Wooden Casket - Solid wood or Veneer

- Eco-friendly Casket - Bamboo

- Custom or Personalized Casket - Unique designs and artwork, to reflect the individual's personality

- Cremation Casket - Usually simpler in construction and materials

- Biodegradable Caskets - Designed to break down naturally over time, suitable for green or natural burials

- Renting a Casket - Some funeral homes offer casket rental options for services with cremation following the viewing or ceremony

6. Funerary Attire: Garments of Remembrance:

The chosen clothing should reflect your personality, preferences and the tone of the funeral service. Here are some considerations:

- Formal Attire - Black or dark-colored clothing, e.g.: suits and dresses

- Cultural and Religious Attire - Some cultures may have specific colors or traditional garments associated with mourning

- Military or Organizational Uniforms

- Individualized Elements - Incorporating preferred accessories, colors and even the wedding suit

7. Harmonizing the Details: A Tapestry of Personal Touches:

7.1 Grave Inscription:

If you opt for burial (4.1), you can choose your preferred words or verses from the holy book to be etched onto your grave, and also have the opportunity to design the grave.

7.2 Photo Displays:

Arrange for the installation of photo displays or a slideshow that commemorates your life and relationships, to be showcased either during the wake or at subsequent prayer gatherings. You may attach a separate note or link for these details.

7.3 Digital Memorial:

Digital Memorial Preference: Specify if you would like an online commemoration or memorial page on social media platforms, and provide necessary details or instructions.

8. Eulogies and Tributes Coordination:

You can include a personal letter or poem for your loved ones, to be read by the speaker after the eulogies and tributes proceedings.

Advance Directive Form (ADFs) / Advance Care Planning (ACP) – Voices from Beyond

In the symphony of life, where our narratives intertwine with uncertainty, the chapter on Advance Directive Forms (ADFs) and Advance Care Planning (ACP) becomes a poignant crescendo. Here, we embark on a journey to give our voices resonance beyond the realms of incapacitation, shaping our medical choices and preserving our autonomy.

The global landscape of ADFs and ACPs unfolds as a tapestry of diverse practices and legal nuances. In the Western realms, legal frameworks recognize and endorse these profound documents. Yet, even within these territories, the specifics vary, dictated by state or provincial jurisdiction.

Wherever we stand on this global stage, discussions on end-of-life care and respect for patient autonomy echo through the corridors of cultural diversity. Initiatives encourage dialogue on end-of-life preferences, weaving a tapestry of cultural and legal evolution.

As the global healthcare landscape evolves, it is crucial to acknowledge the dynamic nature of regulations. Seeking professional guidance in this symphony of choices harmonizes decisions with nuanced legal frameworks, ensuring accuracy tailored to your specific location.

This template, embracing a durable power of attorney for health care and a living will, becomes the ink that inscribes your choices onto the pages of tomorrow. It is an instrument of empowerment, enabling you to designate a trusted individual to shape your medical decisions if the future renders you voiceless.

Regular Updates Reminder:

Recognizing the ever-changing dynamics of life, it is crucial to understand that our preferences, perspectives and circumstances evolve. Regularly revisiting and updating your Advance Directive Forms (ADFs) and Advance Care Planning (ACP) document is a responsibility and an act of self-awareness. Major life events such as marriages, births or health-related changes may require revisions to ensure that your wishes align with your current circumstances.

Digital Copies Note:

Keep secure digital copies of your ADFs and ACP documents in a protected online storage platform. This guarantees easy access for you and provides a streamlined avenue for designated individuals when needed. Whether for an emergency situation or routine review, maintaining a digital copy enhances the efficiency of the process, ensuring a swift connection between your preferences and the timely execution of medical decisions.

Definitions to Know:

Understanding the terminology associated with Advance Directives is pivotal in making informed decisions. Here are key definitions to empower your grasp of this vital subject:

1. **Advance Directive:** A written document that communicates an individual's medical treatment preferences for a future scenario where they cannot express these wishes.

2. **Artificial Nutrition and Hydration:** The administration of food and water through a tube to sustain a person's nutritional needs.

3. **Autopsy:** An examination performed on a deceased body to determine the cause of death.

4. **Comfort Care:** Supportive care aimed at keeping a person comfortable without the expectation of recovery. It includes activities like bathing, turning and maintaining moisture on the lips.

5. **CPR (Cardiopulmonary Resuscitation):** Medical interventions to revive a person's breathing or heartbeat. It may involve chest compressions, intubation or other treatments.

6. **Durable Power of Attorney for Health Care:** An advance directive appointing someone to make medical decisions on

behalf of an individual if they become incapable of making their own decisions.

7. **Life-sustaining Treatment:** Any medical intervention employed to prevent a person from dying. Examples include a breathing machine, CPR, artificial nutrition and hydration.

8. **Living Will:** An advance directive specifying the medical treatments an individual desires or rejects when they are unable to communicate their wishes.

9. **Organ and Tissue Donation:** Permission for the removal of organs or tissues after death for transplantation or experimental purposes.

10. **Persistent Vegetative State:** A state of unconsciousness with no hope of regaining awareness, even with medical intervention.

11. **Terminal Condition:** An incurable injury or illness that doctors anticipate will lead to death, even with medical treatment. Life-sustaining treatments may only prolong the dying process in the presence of a terminal condition.

For a comprehensive and practical guide, please refer to the sample template in Part B: Workbook. This workbook provides a structured format for organizing your preferences, ensuring clarity and facilitating efficient communication with healthcare providers and designated decision-makers.

Chapter VI

The Art of Will Writing – Legacy in Ink

The Importance of Having a Will

Crafting a will is not just a legal formality; it is an act of profound foresight and care. Without it, the symphony of your life's assets may be conducted by the impersonal hand of state laws, potentially straying far from the melody you wish to compose for your loved ones. This chapter delves into the significance of a will, illuminating the path toward clarity and control over the inheritance you bequeath.

Steps to Write a Will

Creating a will can be straightforward with the right guidance. This section delineates a step-by-step blueprint for drafting a will, from asset identification to beneficiary designation and executor selection. Practical advice and considerations are provided for a smooth navigation through each stage.

Legal Requirements

Understanding the legal prerequisites for crafting a will is essential in the global context, considering the varied legal landscapes across jurisdictions. While specifics may differ, this section provides overarching principles to guide the process. Emphasizing the importance of aligning your will with local standards, it offers general insights to fortify enforceability and reduce the potential for disputes. Recognizing the global diversity in legal frameworks, seeking professional advice specific to your jurisdiction is recommended, ensuring a precise and legally sound execution of your final wishes.

Choosing an Executor

In the orchestration of your legacy, the role of the executor is pivotal. This section elucidates the responsibilities bestowed upon this key figure and provides sagacious recommendations for selecting an individual capable of navigating the intricacies of your estate with respect and diligence. The choice of an executor is the linchpin that transforms intentions into reality.

Updating Your Will

As the chapters of your life unfold, so should the verses of your will. Life's evolution necessitates a dynamic document. This section underscores the importance of frequent reviews and amendments to ensure your will aligns with your current desires and circumstances. In the ever-changing narrative, your will remains a relevant and precise reflection of your intentions.

Information Precision

Ensure precision in all details by verifying that all information is accurate and up-to-date.

Transparent Communication

Facilitate transparent communication by discussing your wishes with your executor, family and a legal professional.

Secure Accessibility

Ensure secure accessibility by storing this document in a safe location while providing copies to your executor and a trusted family member or friend.

Definitions to Know:

1. **Executor:** An individual appointed to carry out the wishes as outlined in your Will.

2. **Asset:** Any possession with monetary value, such as property, stocks, bonds or bank accounts.

3. **Beneficiary:** An individual or organization that will receive assets or property as specified in your Will.

4. **Guardian:** An individual appointed to care for minor children in the event of your passing.

For a comprehensive guide, please refer to the sample template in Part B: Workbook. This resource provides a structured format for organizing preferences, ensuring clarity and fostering effective communication with legal professionals and designated executors.

Crucially, it verifies the accuracy and legality of your will document, ensuring compliance with state/country regulations— an indispensable step for a legally sound representation of your final wishes.

Chapter VII

Bequeathing Memories – Crafting My Legacy and Personal Belongings Distribution

Leaving a legacy is a beautiful way to continue impacting the lives of loved ones and even communities after one's passing.

In this chapter, include memorial notes to evoke cherished memories among your loved ones after your passing. These notes can encompass various heartfelt elements like family recipes, traditions, inspirational quotes, personal insights, book recommendations and more. Consider preserving your sentiments through audio or video recordings for a lasting impact.

Here are some inspiring examples and ideas that you might want to contemplate as a way of showcasing the legacy you wish to impart.

1. **Family Heirloom Story:**

    Sarah inherited her grandmother's vintage locket, passed down through generations. Inside the locket, she found a small note with a heartfelt message from her grandmother.

The locket not only keeps her connected to her grandmother but also reminds her of her family's history and values.

2. **Personal Memoirs:**

John always admired his father's resilience and wisdom. Before passing, his father wrote a memoir recounting his life experiences, lessons learned and the values he cherished. This memoir became a cherished guide for John and a way to keep his father's memory alive.

3. **Community Scholarship Fund:**

Mr. and Mrs. Thompson were passionate about education. They established a scholarship fund in their local community to support students in need. Their legacy continues to provide educational opportunities for many, year after year.

4. **Recipe Book Legacy:**

Maria's mother was known for her exceptional cooking. Before passing, she compiled a recipe book containing all of the family's favorite dishes. Now, the family gathers every Sunday to cook a meal from the book, keeping her memory alive through these shared experiences.

5. **Digital Legacy:**

Tom was a photographer who captured the beauty of his hometown. Before passing, he created a digital portfolio of his work. His family later discovered the portfolio and decided to share it online. Now, Tom's breathtaking photographs continue to inspire others and celebrate the beauty of his community.

6. Memorial Garden:

In memory of their daughter who loved nature, a couple created a beautiful public garden. The garden is not only a peaceful place for reflection but also a community haven that embodies their daughter's love for nature and continues to touch the lives of many.

7. Personalized Letters:

Emma wrote individual letters to her children and grandchildren, to be opened on special occasions. Each letter contained her blessings, anecdotes and advice. These letters have become a source of comfort, wisdom and a tangible connection to Emma on significant life milestones.

8. Handcrafted Gifts:

James, a skilled woodworker, handcrafted beautiful wooden toys for his grandchildren. These toys are not only cherished keepsakes but a reminder of the hours and love James invested in creating something special for each of them.

Acknowledgement and Thank You

Approaching the final pages of **Part, A – Guidebook of Soulful Departures - A Journal on End-of-Life Readiness**, I want to express my sincere gratitude for embarking on this introspective journey with me. Delving into the topic of death with foresight requires courage, and your commitment to preparation is a profound act of consideration toward yourself and your loved ones, providing a guiding light during challenging times.

Beyond addressing the end, this process is a tribute to the moments leading up to it. Your meticulous planning is a testament to your love and care for those who matter most to you.

As you transition from this chapter to the future, may the peace derived from preparation and the assurance of leaving behind a meaningful legacy accompany you.

Wishing you strength, serenity and an abundance of joy in all the days that lie ahead.

Now, turn the page to **Part, B – Workbook of Soulful Departures - A Journal on End- of-Life Readiness**, where your thoughtful preparations take a practical form. Let's continue this journey, transforming insights into actionable plans for a soulful departure.

Part B: Work Book

Susan David

Contents

Journal Owner – Who am I?

Note: The information listed below is essential or standard for your executor, but you have the option to offer additional details to facilitate the process. For instance, in the Insurance Details column, you may choose to include your agent's contact details if desired.

A. Personal Details:

Full Legal Name:	
Date of Birth:	
International Passport Number:	
National Identification Number:	
Current Residential Address:	

Personal Mobile Number:	
Personal Email Address:	
Social Security Details (Applicable for Malaysians): Employees Provident Fund (EPF) Number: Social Security Organization (SOCSO) Number:	
Personal Insurance Provider Name: Review and update beneficiaries on insurance policies. (attach as an annexure to the original Will document for reference)	
Policy Number (if any):	
Current Employer Name:	
Current Employer HR Contact Details:	

B. Important Contacts:

Provide a comprehensive list of crucial contacts, including family members, lawyers, financial advisors and healthcare providers, facilitating communication and coordination during the execution of your plans.

Spouse Details:

Full Legal Name:	
Contact Details:	

Children Details:

Full Legal Name:	
Contact Details:	
Full Legal Name:	
Contact Details:	
Full Legal Name:	
Contact Details:	

Full Legal Name:	
Contact Details:	
Full Legal Name:	
Contact Details:	
Full Legal Name:	
Contact Details:	
Full Legal Name:	
Contact Details:	
Full Legal Name:	
Contact Details:	
Full Legal Name:	
Contact Details:	

Support System Mapping: Guardian / Best Friend Details/ Tribe:

Tribe refers to different group of friends from school, college, work, clubs etc. where a representative detail is required for communication purposes.

Full Legal Name:	
Relationship:	
Contacts Details:	
Institute Engaged (Name):	
Full Legal Name:	
Relationship:	
Contacts Details:	
Institute Engaged (Name):	
Full Legal Name:	
Relationship:	
Contacts Details:	
Institute Engaged (Name):	

Full Legal Name:	
Relationship:	
Contacts Details:	
Institute Engaged (Name):	
Full Legal Name:	
Relationship:	
Contacts Details:	
Institute Engaged (Name):	
Full Legal Name:	
Relationship:	
Contacts Details:	
Institute Engaged (Name):	

Full Legal Name:	
Relationship:	
Contacts Details:	
Institute Engaged (Name):	
Full Legal Name:	
Relationship:	
Contacts Details:	
Institute Engaged (Name):	

C. Medical Information:

Blood	O +	O -	A +	A -	B +	B -	AB +	AB -
Group								

Other information like allergies, medication lists, chronic diseases, immunization history etc.

D. Important **Documents:**

Ensure thorough organization and easy accessibility of essential documents to facilitate the smooth execution of your wishes after your passing. Specify the location where these documents are stored.

Location of **Primary Documents:**

Original Copy of Official Will Document	
Original Copy of Advance Directive Form / Advance Care Planning (if any)	
Password Sheet (securely stored)	
Original Copy of National Identification Card	
Copy of National Identification Card	
Original Copy of International Passport	
Copy of International Passport	

Printed Copy of Social Security Fund Nominees / Beneficiary Details Review and update beneficiaries on Social Security Fund. (attach as an annexure to the original Will document for reference)	
Original Copy of Personal Insurance Policies (if any)	
Original Copies of Bank Mortgage Documents	
Original Copies of other Financial Investment Documents (shares, unit trust, crypto-currency etc.) Review and update beneficiaries on Financial Investment. (attach as an annexure to the original Will document for reference)	

Company-owned Contracts / Documents	
Children's Documentation (Birth Certificate / National Identification Card, Medical Records, School Records, Certificates etc.) Note: Children below 18 years old	
Marriage Certificates	
Divorce Documents	

Location of **Supplementary Documents:**

Original Copy of Birth Certificate	
Original Copies of Education Certifications	
Medical History Reports (including organ donor card, blood donation book etc.)	
Current Employer Offer Letter	

Vehicle Records	
Pet License and Medical Records	
Tax Returns	

E. Where to Find My...:

Please mention where the related documents (if any) are stored.

House Keys (including spare keys)	
Vehicle Keys (including spare keys)	
Wallet / Purse / Card Holders	
Safe Deposit / Jewelry Box	

Memory Box	
Arts / Collectible Items	

F. My Pets Information (if any):

- Review and update beneficiaries on Pet caretaker. (attach as an annexure to the original Will document for reference)

- If you have many pets, kindly utilize the additional sheet located at the end of this journal for their inclusion.

Pet Name	
Beneficiary / Caretaker (optional, you may choose to specify here or directly within the Will document)	
Other Details. E.g.: Insurance Policies or Savings Accounts registered in the pet's name	

Optional: An image or video links of your pets.	

G. My Estate Custodian:

- **Confidential Information:** Please refrain from sharing sensitive data, such as bank login credentials, in this session.

- If you have multiple properties, kindly utilize the additional sheet located at the end of this journal for their inclusion.

Property Name	
Property Address	
Financial Institution / Corporate Affiliation (Name and Branch)	
Monthly Mortgage Payment	
Home Mortgage Account Number	

Optional: An image or video links of your properties.	

H. My Vehicle:

- **Confidential Information:** Please refrain from sharing sensitive data, such as bank login credentials, in this session.

- If you have multiple vehicles, kindly utilize the additional sheet located at the end of this journal for their inclusion.

Vehicle Registration Number / Model	
Financial Institution / Corporate Affiliation (Name and Branch)	
Monthly Mortgage Payment	
Vehicle Mortgage Account Number	
Optional: An image or video links of your vehicles.	

I. My Banking Details:

Confidential Information: Please refrain from sharing sensitive data, such as bank login credentials, in this session.

Credit Card Account Details / Bank	Bank: Account Number: Bank: Account Number: Bank: Account Number:
Savings Account Details / Bank	Bank: Account Number: Bank: Account Number: Bank: Account Number:

Current Account Details / Bank	Bank: Account Number: Bank: Account Number: Bank: Account Number:
Fixed Deposit Account Details / Bank	Bank: Account Number: Bank: Account Number: Bank: Account Number:

Joint Account Details / Bank	Bank: Account Number: Bank: Account Number: Bank: Account Number:
Home Mortgage Account Details / Bank	Bank: Account Number: Bank: Account Number: Bank: Account Number:

Vehicle Mortgage Account Details / Bank	Bank: Account Number: Bank: Account Number: Bank: Account Number:
Personal Loan Account Details / Bank	Bank: Account Number: Bank: Account Number: Bank: Account Number:

Bank Safe Box Details / Bank	Bank: Account Number: Bank: Account Number: Bank: Account Number:
Other Investment Account Details (applicable in your respective country)	Bank: Account Number: Bank: Account Number: Bank: Account Number:

J. Services to Close and Cancel:

Confidential Information: Please refrain from sharing sensitive data, such as bank login credentials, in this session.

List down subscriptions/memberships with automated debit arrangements. For additional subscriptions, utilize the supplementary sheet located at the end of this journal.

Subscriptions / Memberships	YES (name the subscriptions)	NO
Primary Gmail Account (registered for all financial related matters)		
Mobile Subscription		
Internet Subscription		
Utilities – Electric		
Utilities – Water		
Television Subscription (Amazon Prime, Disney+, Netflix, Apple / Android TV etc.)		
Home Security - Alarm & CCTV		

Home Appliances – Water Filter, Air Purifier, Smart Home Appliances etc.		
Digital Payment (Google Pay, Apple Pay, Samsung Pay etc.)		
Crypto-currency		
Gym / Sports Club Membership		
Premium Car Wash Membership		
LinkedIn (Premier)		
Spotify (Premier)		
YouTube (Premier)		
Newspaper		
Other Subscriptions (Magazines, AI Tools, Learning Portals etc.)		

Active Social Media Subscriptions		
Kindly state who should have the access to the below listed social media accounts and what should be done with each account.		
Facebook		
Instagram		
WhatsApp		
Twitter		
TikTok		
Snapchat		
eBay		
Pinterest		
Telegram		
Other Local Social Media Platforms		
Other Online Shopping Platforms		

K. Digital Assets:

Please turn to Chapter II: Journal Owner – Who am I? under subsection 'K. Digital Asset' in Part A: Guide Book for a comprehensive framework meticulously designed to guide you on securely unlocking and transferring your digital assets. This section provides insights into crafting secure access instructions tailored to your specific needs.

Underline the critical importance of furnishing secure access instructions for these assets, while exercising caution against sharing sensitive information, such as written passwords or password sheets, within this journal. This practice ensures the utmost confidentiality and security for your digital assets.

Outlined below is a sample detailing key information required for documenting access instructions. Subsequently, these details can be organized using the concepts introduced in Chapter III: Password Sheet.

Type of Digital Assets	Name of the Application	Access Instructions	Link / Website	Password / Security Phrase / Picture
E.g.:				
Digital Portfolio	Dribbble	Two-factor authentication (2FA) has been enabled.	www. dribbble. com	Password: ABCD1234 Picture: Apple Security Phrase: Sunflower
Additional Notes:				

Chapter III

Password Sheet – Keys to the Virtual Kingdom

Kindly refer to Chapter III: Password Sheet - Keys to the Virtual Kingdom in Part A: Guide Book for an exhaustive framework of concepts meticulously crafted to aid you in documenting tailored solutions that harmonize with your distinct requirements. **It is strongly recommended to refrain from disseminating any written passwords or password sheets within this journal.**

Presented below is a sample checklist enumerating items necessitating password protection, categorized according to risk levels and objectives, for your perusal.

Risk: High

Objective: To facilitate efficient data retrieval and ensure data security.

Items	User Name	Password	Pin Code / Security Phrase
Personal Emails			
Personal Mobile			
Company Mobile			
Personal Laptop			
Company Laptop			
Personal Tab / iPad			
Company Tab / iPad			
Jewelry Box			
Memory Box			

Risk: High

Objective: To cease monthly payments promptly and unsubscribe without delay.

Note: Digital payment and credit/debit card details are to be immediately removed from the registered mobile applications.

Items	User Name	Password	Payment Frequency (Monthly / Annually)	Payment Method (Bank Transfer / Credit Card etc.)	Auto Debit (Yes / No)	Remarks
Digital Payment (Google Pay, Apple Pay, Samsung Pay etc.)						

Bank Safe Box (Specify the bank name)					
Utilities – Electric					
Utilities – Water					
Mobile Subscription					

Internet Subscription					
Television Subscription					
Amazon Prime					
Netflix					

Maintenance fees and sinking fund			
Property Management Office	Home Security – Alarm & CCTV	Home Appliances – Water Filter, Air Purifier etc.	Gym / Sports Club Membership

LinkedIn (Premier)						
Spotify (Premier)						
YouTube (Premier)						

Risk: High

Objective: Financial Liabilities, Savings and Investments.

Items (Specify the bank name)	User Name	Password	Payment Frequency (Monthly / Annually)	Payment Method (Bank Transfer / Credit Card etc.)	Auto Debit (Yes / No)	Remarks
Savings Account	Bank: User Name:					

Current Account	Bank: User Name:					
Fixed Deposit Account	Bank: User Name:					
Home Mortgage Account	Bank: User Name:					
Vehicle Mortgage Account	Bank: User Name:					

Personal Loan Account	Bank:					
	User Name:					
Joint Account	Bank:					
	User Name:					
Credit Card Balance Transfer	Bank:					
	User Name:					
Crypto- currency	Bank:					
	User Name:					

	Bank:	User Name:			
Social Security Portal					
Personal Insurance Portal	Bank:	User Name:			
Amanah Saham Nasional Berhad Account	Bank:	User Name:			
Public Mutual Investment	Bank:	User Name:			

	Bank:				
Kenanga Investment	User Name:				
Other Investment Account Details	Bank:				
	User Name:				

Risk: Medium

Objective: Miscellaneous Records from Various Sources with No Commercial Implications.

Items	User Name	Password	Remarks
Current Employer Medical Insurance Portal			
Vehicle Company Application			Maintenance and Service Appointment
Government Related Applications E.g.: MySejahtera (for Malaysians)			

Risk: Low

Objective: As a data protection measure, the company should deactivate social media accounts by default when registered email addresses are deactivated upon the account holder's passing.

Items	User Name	Password	Remarks
Facebook			
Facebook Messenger			
WhatsApp			
Instagram			
Twitter			
TikTok			
Telegram			
Snapchat			
Pinterest			

Items	User Name	Password	Remarks
LinkedIn (Basic)			
YouTube (Basic)			
Spotify (Basic)			
Tumblr			
Others			

Risk: Low

Objective: The purchase is contingent upon the active status of the credit card and becomes void upon cancellation of the credit card.

Note: Please perform a verification to confirm whether the credit/debit card details have been successfully removed.

Items	User Name	Password	Remarks
eBay			
PayPal			

Items	User Name	Password	Remarks
Amazon			
AliExpress			
Flipkart			
Etsy			
Lazada			
Shopee			
Grab			
FoodPanda			
Fave			
Carousell			
Mudah.my			
Touch N Go			

Funeral Planning – A Symphony of Final Wishes

This is a general funeral planning guide and does not adhere to any specific religious practices. Therefore, please complete only the relevant sections, as they serve as a reference for executers to facilitate the arrangement of your funeral.

1. **Designate a Responsible Individual to Contact Religious Leaders and Funeral Services Company:**

2. **Harmony in Funeral Services: Crafting the Farewell:**

3. **Venue Selection: Choosing the Stage for the Final Act:**

4. **Resting in Peace: Burial or Cremation:**

   Burial and cremation are the two primary methods for laying a person to rest. Each option has its own set of rituals, costs and considerations.

4.1 If Choosing Burial, please specify:

For a New Lot	(YES / NO)
OR pick your preferred existing grave (if any). For example: To be interred in my late grandmother's grave in my hometown	

4.2 If Opting for Cremation, please indicate your preference for the ashes:

5. Casket Choices: Crafting the Vessel for the Voyage Beyond:

6. Funerary Attire: Garments of Remembrance:

7. Harmonizing the Details: A Tapestry of Personal Touches:

7.1 Grave Inscription: Option 4.1 (Burial)

7.2 Photo Displays:

Links:

Notes:

7.3 Digital Memorial:

8. Eulogies and Tributes Coordination:

You can include a personal letter or poem for your loved ones, to be read by the speaker after the eulogies and tributes proceedings.

•

Advance Directive Form (ADFs) / Advance Care Planning (ACP) – Voices from Beyond

Legal Disclaimer:

It is important to consult with legal professionals when filling out this section of the journal.

Instructions:

Read each section carefully. Before you fill out the form, talk to the person you want to name, to make sure that he/she understands your wishes and is willing to take the responsibility. Write your initials in the blank spaces before the choices you want to make. Write your initials only beside the choices you want under Part 1, 2 and 3 of this form. Your advance directive. should be valid for whatever part(s) you fill in, as long as it is properly signed.

Add any special instructions in the blank spaces provided. You can write additional comments on a separate sheet of paper, but you should write on this form that there are additional pages to your advance directive. Sign the form and have it witnessed. Give copies to your doctor, your nurse, the person you name to make your medical decisions for you, people in your family and anyone else who might be involved in your care. Discuss your advance directive with them.

Understand that you may change or cancel this document at any time.

Complete this portion of Advance Directive Form

I, _______________________________________[Your Full Name], _______________________________________[Your National Identification Number], born on ___________________________[Your Date of Birth], residing at ____

____
_______________________________________[Your Address], being of sound mind, write this document as a directive regarding my medical care.

PART 1.
My Durable Power of Attorney for Health Care

I appoint this person to make decisions about my medical care if there ever comes a time when I cannot make those decisions myself. I want the person I have appointed, my doctors, my family and others to be guided by the decisions I have made in the parts of the form that follow.

Full Legal Name:	
Relationship to You:	
National Identification Number:	
Personal Mobile Number:	
Personal Mailing Address:	
Current Residential Address:	

If the person above cannot or will not make decisions for me, I appoint this person:

Full Legal Name:	
Relationship to You:	
National Identification Number:	
Personal Mobile Number:	
Personal Mailing Address:	

Current Residential Address:	

I have not appointed anyone to make health care decisions for me in any other document.

PART 2.
My Living Will

These are my wishes for my future medical care if there ever comes a time when I cannot make these decisions for myself.

A. These are my wishes if I have a terminal condition.

Life-sustaining treatments

☐ I do not want life-sustaining treatment (including CPR) started. If life-sustaining treatments are started, I want them stopped.

☐ I want to receive the following life-sustaining treatments that my doctors think is best for me.

    ☐ Cardiopulmonary resuscitation (CPR)

    ☐ Mechanical ventilation

    ☐ Dialysis

    ☐ Nutritional and hydration assistance

    ☐ Antibiotics or antiviral medications

- ☐ Any other treatment deemed necessary by medical professionals

☐ Other wishes ______________________________

____

Artificial nutrition and hydration

☐ I do not want artificial nutrition and hydration started if they would be the main treatments keeping me alive. If artificial nutrition and hydration are started, I want them stopped.

☐ I want artificial nutrition and hydration even if they are the main treatments keeping me alive.

☐ Other wishes ______________________________

____

Comfort care

☐ I want to be kept as comfortable and free of pain as possible, even if such care prolongs my dying or shortens my life.

☐ Other wishes ______________________________

____

B. These are my wishes if I am ever in a persistent vegetative state.

Life-sustaining treatments

☐ I do not want life-sustaining treatments (including CPR) started. If life-sustaining treatments are started, I want them stopped.

☐ I want to receive the following life-sustaining treatments that my doctors think is best for me.

   ☐ Cardiopulmonary resuscitation (CPR)

   ☐ Mechanical ventilation

   ☐ Dialysis

   ☐ Nutritional and hydration assistance

   ☐ Antibiotics or antiviral medications

   ☐ Any other treatment deemed necessary by medical professionals

☐ Other wishes ____

____

Artificial nutrition and hydration

☐ I do not want artificial nutrition and hydration started if they would be the main treatments keeping me alive. If artificial nutrition and hydration are started, I want them stopped.

☐ I want artificial nutrition and hydration even if they are the main treatments keeping me alive.

☐ Other wishes ____

____

Comfort care

☐ I want to be kept as comfortable and free of pain as possible, even if such care prolongs my dying or shortens my life.

☐ Other wishes ____

____

C. Specific Medical Instructions:

Include any other specific instructions about your medical treatment at the end of life.

____

____

____

____

____

____

____

D. Other directions

You have the right to be involved in all decisions about your medical care, even those not dealing with terminal conditions or persistent vegetative states. If you have wishes not covered in other parts of this document, please indicate them below.

PART 3.
Other Wishes

A. Organ donation

☐   I do not wish to donate any of my organs or tissues.

☐   I want to donate all of my organs and tissues.

☐   I only want to donate these organs and tissues:

ORGANS	YES	NO	REMARKS
Kidney			
Liver			
Heart			
Lungs			
Pancreas			
Small Intestine			
Bone Marrow			
Stomach			
Eyes			
Skin			
Bone Tissue			

☐ Other wishes _______________________________________

____

B. Autopsy

☐ I do not want an autopsy.

☐ I agree to an autopsy if my doctors wish it.

☐ Other wishes _______________________________________

____

C. Other statements about your medical care

If you wish to say more about any of the choices you have made or if you have any other statements to make about your medical care, you may do so on a separate piece of paper or the official Will document. If you do so, put here the number of pages you are adding:

For example: List any facilities or home-care services you prefer.

PART 4.
Signatures

You and two witnesses must sign this document before it will be legal.

A. Your signature

By my signature below, I show that I understand the purpose and the effect of this document.

Signature	
Date:	
National Identification Number:	

B. Your witnesses' signatures

I believe the person who has signed this advance directive to be of sound mind, that he/she signed or acknowledged this advance directive in my presence, and that he/she appears not to be acting under pressure, duress, fraud or undue influence. I am not related to the person making this advance directive by blood, marriage or adoption nor, to the best of my knowledge, am I named in his/her Will. I am not the person appointed in this advance directive. I am not a health care provider or an employee of a health care provider who is now, or has been in the past, responsible for the care of the person making this advance directive.

Witness #1:

Signature	
Date:	
National Identification Number:	

Witness #2:

Signature	
Date:	
National Identification Number:	

Chapter VI

The Art of Will Writing – Legacy in Ink

Legal Disclaimer:

It is important to consult with legal professionals when filling out this section of the journal.

I, ________________________________[Your Full Name], ____________________________[Your National Identification Number], born on________________________[Your Date of Birth], residing at ____ ________________________________[Your Address], being of sound mind and disposing memory, do hereby declare this to be my last will and testament, revoking all prior wills and codicils.

In the following sections, put the initials of your name in the blank spaces by the choices you want.

PART 1. Personal Representative / Executor

I appoint this person to serve as the Executor of my estate. The Executor shall have the authority to execute and carry out the decisions, bequests and instructions set forth in the parts of this Will that follow.

Full Legal Name:	
Relationship to You:	
National Identification Number:	
Personal Mobile Number:	
Personal Mailing Address:	
Current Residential Address:	

If the person above is unable or unwilling to act, I appoint this person as the alternate Executor, with the same authority to execute the decisions outlined herein:

Full Legal Name:	
Relationship to You:	
National Identification Number:	

Personal Mobile Number:	
Personal Mailing Address:	
Current Residential Address:	

PART 2. Asset Distribution:

I give, devise and bequeath all of my property and assets, of whatever nature and wherever situated, to the following individuals or entities:

Real Estate Properties	Beneficiary	Percentage of Allocation	Relationship

Bank Accounts / Investments / Retirement Fund	Beneficiary	Percentage of Allocation	Relationship

Valuables	Beneficiary	Percentage of Allocation	Relationship
E.g.: Jewelry, Art, Collectibles etc.			

Insurance	Beneficiary	Percentage of Allocation	Relationship

If any of the above-named beneficiaries predecease me, their share shall be divided equally among the surviving beneficiaries.

PART 3. Debts and Liabilities:

Mortgage and Loan	Beneficiary	Relationship
E.g.: Home, Vehicle, Personal Loan, Credit Card etc.		

PART 4. Guardian for Minor Children (if applicable):

I appoint this person as the Guardian of my minor children:

Full Legal Name:	
Relationship to You:	
National Identification Number:	
Personal Mobile Number:	
Personal Mailing Address:	
Current Residential Address:	

If the person above unable or unwilling to act, I appoint this person as the alternate Guardian:

Full Legal Name:	
Relationship to You:	
National Identification Number:	
Personal Mobile Number:	
Personal Mailing Address:	
Current Residential Address:	

PART 5: Residuary Clause:

I direct that any property not specifically devised or bequeathed in this Will shall be distributed according to the laws of intestate succession of the [Your Jurisdiction].

PART 6: Special Instructions and Additional Provision:

If you wish to;

- specify any additional instructions about specific assets, sentimental items or conditions for beneficiaries OR

- include any preferences or wishes regarding the management or distribution of specific assets you may do so on a separate piece of paper. If you do so, put here the number of pages you are adding:

____

For example: I wish to provide special instructions and additional information on my pet caretakers.

PART 7. Signatures

You and two witnesses must sign this document before it will be legal.

1. **Your signature**

    By my signature below, I show that I understand the purpose and the effect of this document.

Signature	
Date:	
National Identification Number:	

2. **Your witnesses' signatures**

    I believe the person who has signed this Will to be of sound mind, that he/she signed or acknowledged this Will in my presence, and that he/she appears not to be acting under pressure, duress, fraud or undue influence. I am not related to the person making this Will by blood, marriage or adoption nor, to the best of my knowledge, am I named in his/her Will. I am not the person appointed in this Will. I am not a health care provider or an employee of a health care provider who is now or has been in the past, responsible for the care of the person making this Will.

Witness #1:

Signature	
Date:	
National Identification Number:	

Witness #2:

Signature	
Date:	
National Identification Number:	

Chapter VII

Bequeathing Memories – Crafting My Legacy and Personal Belongings Distribution

Chapter VIII

Introspection – Journey into the Self

Reflecting on your emotional landscape involves understanding and acknowledging your feelings, which is a crucial aspect of the planning journey. To guide your introspection, consider the following questions:

- How did you perceive the concept of end-of-life planning throughout this journaling experience?

- What apprehensions or worries arose for you during the contemplation of end-of-life matters?

- What sources of solace or reassurance did you discover to navigate through this introspective journey?

- Concluding Remarks and Farewell Reflections.

Thank You and Feedback

Thank you for embarking on the practical journey through Part B - Workbook of Soulful Departures - A Journal on End-of-Life Readiness. Your commitment in translating insights into actionable plans demonstrates an act of great courage and foresight.

Remember that this process is not just about the end; it is about cherishing the moments leading up to it. Your thoughtful consideration and planning speak volumes about the love and care you have for those around you.

As you have closed preparation of this chapter of your life, I hope you had the peace that came from preparation and the knowledge that you have taken a significant step toward ensuring a meaningful legacy and with this I highly value your feedback on your experience with Soulful Departures.

Please take a moment to share your thoughts via our Google Form  [what do you think?], enabling me to continually enhance the resources and better serve you. Thank you once again for your participation in this essential process. Wishing you clarity, resilience and fulfillment as you navigate this journey towards end-of- life readiness.

If you need any guidance to complete this journal, personalized walk-through services are available for a small fee. Please fill out this Google form [let us do it together], and I will provide appointment slots within 24 hours, considering the time zone variances across the globe.

Supplementary Pages

134

9 798894 153995